The *Magic* Nut A prologue to *The Nutcracker*

Mihail Chemiakin

The *Magic* Nut

A prologue to *The Nutcracker*

Editor
Paola Gribaudo

Cover Design
Marcello Francone

Editorial Coordination
Elena Carotti

Editing
Emily Ligniti

Layout
Monica Temporiti

Translations
Sarah H. de Kay,
from Russian into English

Art photography
Arkady Lvov

Photo credits
V. Baranovsky, pp. 8, 144
S. de Kay, p. 144
M. Pandoursky, p. 9
I. Tsvetkova, p. 7

The Magic Nut premiered at the
Mariinsky Theater,
St. Petersburg, May 14, 2005

Performed by the Mariinsky Ballet

First published in Italy in 2005 by
Skira Editore S.p.A.
Palazzo Casati Stampa
via Torino 61
20123 Milano
Italy
www.skira.net

Printed and bound in Italy.
First edition

ISBN 88-7624-376-3

Distributed in North America by
Rizzoli International Publications,
Inc., 300 Park Avenue South,
New York, NY 10010.
Distributed elsewhere in the world
by Thames and Hudson Ltd., 181a
High Holborn, London WC1V
7QX, United Kingdom.

Table of Contents

Балет "Щелкунчик".

I Действие. 1ая Картина.

Королевский зал.

Король, Королева, придворные.
Все волнуются, ждут рождения
Принцессы. Вбегают радостные
повивальные бабки — Принцесса
родилась! Король танцует от
счастья. Пляшет на одной ноге.
Шут подражает ему. Гости присоединяются.
Танец на одной ноге. (Танец гостей.) (?)

Выносят запелёнутую принцессу.
Король в восторге берёт её в руки.
Умилённо показывает гостям.
Ласково играет с ней. Щелкунчик
неожиданно кусает его за палец.
Вдобавок мочится сквозь пелёнки.
Король возвращает ребёнка
Королеве, та передаёт —
служанкам. Принцессу уносят
Король хлопает в ладоши —

Приглашает всех на
Колбасный праздничный ужин

A page from the libretto of *The Magic Nut*

The Magic Nut

This is the story of the magical Crackatook nut, Princess Pirlipat, and a young man, Herr Drosselmeyer's enchanted nephew. In Hoffman's *Nutcracker* tale, Herr Drosselmeyer tells the heroine Marie (Masha) this story while she is recuperating from the attack of the Rat King and his subjects. The idea of staging the whole Hoffman tale, including the story of Pirlipat and the magic nut, first arose about thirty years after the first production of *The Nutcracker*, when choreographer Fyodor Lopukhov commissioned Shostakovich to write the music. Unfortunately it was right after the composer was savaged by the press for his music for the ballets *Bolt* and *The Limpid Stream*, and Shostakovich backed away from ballet scores.

Many choreographers have attempted to tell the story of the Nutcracker's origins, because without this the ballet's plot is not quite clear. Some have had Drosselmeyer put on a puppet show, which is utterly incomprehensible to the audience; Lopukhov had the Nutcracker approach the audience and tell his story in words. Others have inserted the story of the hard nut and Princess Pirlipat in the beginning of Act II. But I decided to return to Lopukhov's original idea—the creation of new music and finally a whole new ballet for the story of the hard nut, as this plot is complex and demands separate treatment.

In *The Magic Nut* the audience will observe the transformation of young Drosselmeyer into a Nutcracker. His relationship to the rats will be clearer—the audience will see that once upon a time everyone—rats, birds, people—lived together peacefully, until they fell out because the rats ate all the lard in the King's sausages (in my version they steal the sausages whole). This quarrel leads to a series of events that reveal young Drosselmeyer's (the future Nutcracker's) kind heart, and how he nearly became a member of the royal family by breaking the spell on Princess Pirlipat, but then was himself turned into a Nutcracker by the rats. The relationship between the Nutcracker and Herr Drosselmeyer is also clarified. After all, on the one hand the uncle got his nephew into a most unpleasant predicament, but on the other hand only Herr Drosselmeyer knows how to break the rats' evil spells. I hope that the audience will feel sympathy for the kind and unhappy youth and will follow his story in Tchaikovsky's ballet with increased interest and understanding.

Mihail Chemiakin

Composer's Notes

E. T.A. Hoffman's *Tales* amaze the reader with the expression of the mighty conflict between nobility and venality, idealism and cynicism, the spiritual potency of good and the villainous malice of the rat underworld. These themes are present in his tale, *Nutcracker and the Mouse King*. Hoffman's Serapion Brothers were the model for a literary circle in 1920s Petrograd. Among the members of the circle were Zoschenko, Lev Lunets, and my father, Mikhail Slonimsky. Thus it was with great interest and pleasure that I worked on the musical score for Chemiakin's new Hoffman ballet. Worthiness Punished is the theme of *A Tale of a Hard Nut*, in which Herr Drosselmeyer in *Nutcracker and the Mouse King* tells the story of the Nutcracker. Here Drosselmeyer's magnanimous nephew, who has saved Pirlipat from eternal ugliness, is rejected and given up to the rats' curse. In his libretto, Chemiakin emphasized the noble, chivalrous motives of the young man, who loves Pirlipat when she is a pathetic, ugly monster. Not under threat of execution by the capricious King, but out of feelings of empathy and self-sacrifice, the future Prince saves the young Princess. But Pirlipat is no Masha! She turns out to be ungrateful, with a weakness for appearances and power, utterly incapable of rising to self-sacrifice and fidelity in love. And the noble youth remains in the hands of the rats, who have turned the hero into a silly and helpless Nutcracker and celebrate their victory in an orgy of malice. All the guests, the King, and the Princess herself laugh at him, drive him out, and leave him in bitter isolation. How often this sort of thing happens in real life, to us, to our friends and families! The Hoffman tale remains utterly contemporary, however essentially sad that might be . . .

Chemiakin's choreographic libretto seized me with the same depth of thought and unlimited breadth of imagination that are characteristic of his version of *The Nutcracker*. And I happily agreed to compose music for the one-act ballet, worked with enthusiasm, with unfailing inspiration. I did not use any of Tchaikovsky's peerless melodies, for that would have been pretentious. Rather, I composed the musical themes myself, keeping in mind several groups of sound images.

The melodic leitmotifs of the orchestra represent the world of people, of their kind feelings, of sadness and joy, loneliness and love. Various characters of the story are presented in episodes of the orchestration. The organ represents the magic of the kind sorcerer Drosselmeyer. And the purely contemporary insertion of unusual electronic music portrays the evil magic of Krysilda and her rat army. The residents of the Rat kingdom also dance to the sounds and rhythms of "mini-music" and "retro" music, so popular today, parodied as Cervantes parodied the popular chivalrous novels of his time in *Don Quixote*. Has the composer managed to create in the beginning of the twenty-first century a serious symphonic score worthy of librettist-designer-artist Mihail Chemiakin's Hoffmaniana? That, of course, is up to the audience to determine.

Sergei Slonimsky

On *The Magic Nut* and Magic

Magic is a secret and although we can never explain how it happens, we can at least find out why it happens. For me, all the work related to the creation of *The Magic Nut* ballet was magic. E.T.A. Hoffman, Mihail Chemiakin, Sergei Slonimsky, Valery Gergiev, the Mariinsky Theater—all these names taken together already made the magical mixture of which the new fairy-tale ballet was to be born.

Invited as choreographer, I had the task of telling this fairy tale on the stage, in a modern, comprehensible, but also magical language—a tale that would touch the hearts and minds of present-day children and adults. Before my eyes I had, on the one hand, Chemiakin's interesting libretto and his fantastic designs for the sets, costumes, and masques, which compelled me to search for the kind of plasticity that would allow them to come to life naturally on the stage, preserving their Chemiakin spirit. On the other hand—the serious modern symphonic music of Slonimsky and the highly professional ballet troupe of the Mariinsky Theater.

From the onset, I did not think so much of how to stage the ballet but rather, what was it essentially about. Then, drinking big gulps from the magical mixture that fate so graciously offered me, I gradually began to uncover the answer. It was hidden between the different layers of the ballet, the funny and the sad, the grotesque and the romantic. It was Hoffman-Chemiakin, or perhaps even Drosselmeyer, who had to take the viewer by the hand, like little Masha from the fairy tale, and start the journey in the strange world of the eternal struggle between good and evil. The answer also lay in Drosselmeyer's nephew, ready to pass through trial and sacrifice in order to save the ungrateful Princess Pirlipat. Ridiculed and severely punished for his noble character, suffering, he turns to us with his arms open wide and passes to us, in a magical way, his faith in goodness against all odds. To me, this is what lies hidden in the magic nut: the inextinguishable desire to do good, even when life turns its back on us. I would be happy if our ballet succeeds in enchanting the audiences and planting in their hearts a grain of Hoffman's and Chemiakin's magic world.

Donvena Pandoursky

9

The *Magic* Nut

Libretto
Mihail Chemiakin
based on a story by E.T.A. Hoffman

Music
Sergei Slonimsky

Sets, costumes, production
Mihail Chemiakin

Choreography
Donvena Pandoursky

Performed by the
Mariinsky Ballet

(На парике — сверкающая диадемма. в духе короны.)

Орнаменты на платье прожиты золотом и серебром.

Вставить искрящиеся камушки — стеклянные.

Балет „Принцесса Пирлипат.“

Костюм маленькой принцессы Пирлипат.

1-ая Картина.

М. Шемякин

2002 г.

Act I. Scene 1.
The Royal Gardens: Birth of the Princess

The ballet begins with the long-awaited birth of Princess Pirlipat in the bird kingdom. The Princess is born from a Fabergé egg, occasioning great celebration. Her father, the King, dances on one leg, and all the courtiers, gathered for the birth, obligingly follow suit. The courtiers dote on Pirlipat and present her with birthday gifts.

Among the guests at the celebration are members of the rat nobility, whose Queen, Krysilda, considers herself a peer of the bird queen in whose kitchen she lives. Krysilda and Cardinal Kryselieu present the newborn with a Nutcracker doll. The doll frightens Pirlipat and the King hurriedly returns it to the rats to calm the Princess. All the courtiers and guests are invited to a celebratory meal.

балет
"Принцесса
Пирлипат."
(Король.)

М. Шемякин
2002

Король.

Балет "Пролог—
Щелкунчикъ"

I Картина.

М. Шемякин 2001 г.

Балет "Пролог
. Щелкунчикъ"

Король.

Король.

Балет "Пролог—
Щелкунчикъ"

I Картина.

202 г.

15

Эскиз костюма
Королевы

К балету
С. М. Слонимского

„Принцесса
Пирлипат ”

(или
„ Волшебный
орех.”

М. Шемякин
2002 г.

Эскиз костюма
Повивальной
бабки.
Балет С. Слонимского
и К. Самонова
"Принцесса Пирлипат,
или
Наказанное Благородство.
Акт I вст.
Картина I ая

М. Шемякин.
2001 г.
Клавераз
и. у. А.

Эскиз костюма
Придворного лекаря.

Балет С. Слонимского
и С. Самонова
"Принцесса Пирлипат
или
Наказанное
благородство"

Акт I-ый. Картина 1-ая.

М. Шемякин
2002 г.
Клаверак,
U.S.A.

(Движения "Филинообразные.")

20

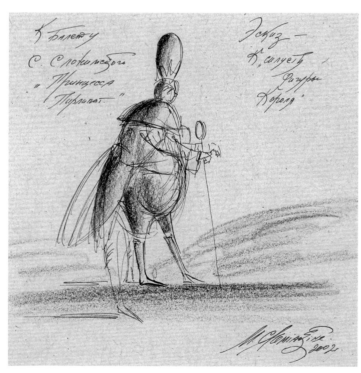

Эскиз костюма гостя короля
Балет С. М. Слонимского
и А. Симонова
«Принцесса Пирлипат
или Наказание благородства.»
Акт Iй. Картина Iя.

М. Шемякин — Каклашот
202г. Клавераи, USA.

2002г.

24

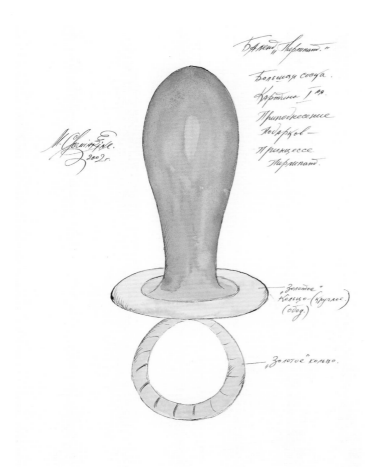

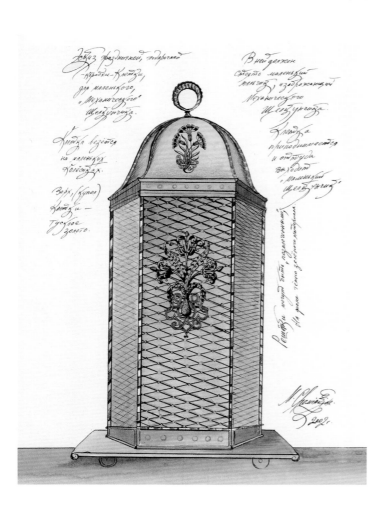

2002 г.

The Royal Pantry

Under the direction of the butler, cooks of various nationalities propose dishes for the banquet. The butler chooses the King's favorite dish, German sausages, and the platters are dispatched to the table. On the way to the table, however, four mischievous rats manage to steal the sausages and make off with them.

Балетъ „Щелкунчикъ."
Картина 2ая
Королевская Кухня.
Эскизъ костюмовъ
Слугъ.
(числомъ 6.)

Белые Перчатки

М. Шемякинъ
2002г.

Эскиз костюма
Повара-Итальянца.
(Балет „Щелкунчик")
Картина 2ая
Кухня короля.

Спагетти.

M. Chemiakine.
2002 г.

Яйцо.

Выпуклый рельеф.
(яйца.)

Яйцо.

Балет „Щелкунчик.“
Картина 2ая
Кухня Короля.

Эскиз костюма
Повара-Китайца.

M. Shemiakine.
2002 г.

Балет „Щелкунчик."

Эскиз костюма

Повара-Немца.
(Колбасник.)

Картина II ая

(Королевская кухня.)

(Вид со спины.)

Балет "Щелкунчик"
Картина 2я
Королевская кухня.

Эсказ костюма
Мажордома.

М. Chemiakine.
2002 г.

44

Балет „Пирлипат."

Картина 2ая

Кухня Короля.

Эскиз костюма

Мажордома.

Бархат.

М. Шемякин.
2002г.

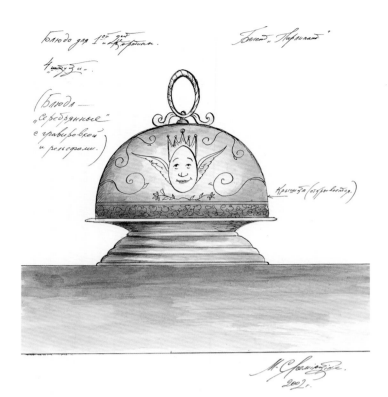

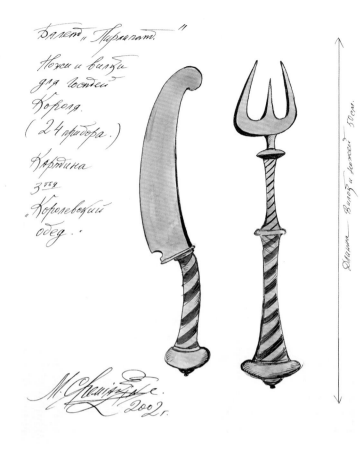

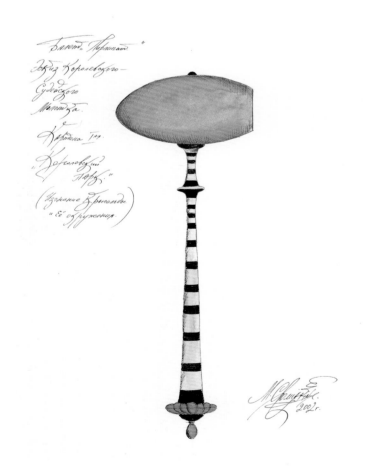

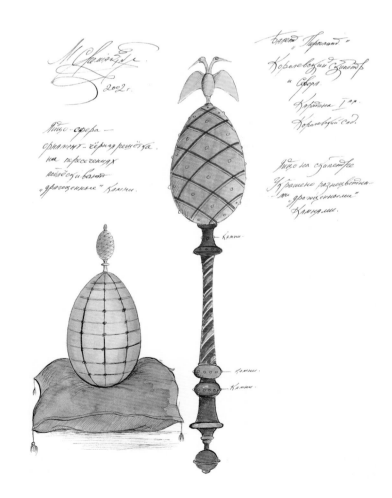

The Royal Gardens: The Banquet

The table is set for the celebration of Pirlipat's birth. Among the guests are the bird courtiers and the rat Queen Krysilda, Cardinal Kryselieu, and some members of the rat aristocracy. Herr Drosselmeyer, the King's sorcerer, arrives with his nephew. Young Drosselmeyer charms the ladies of the court by cracking nuts.

The servants arrive with platters of sausage, but when they uncover the dishes, they are empty. The King is enraged. He demands to know who is responsible and orders Herr Drosselmeyer to explain what has happened. After brief reflection, Drosselmeyer points to the rats. The King immediately exiles Krysilda and sentences the rat aristocrats to execution.

The Dungeon

The condemned rats are led to the gallows, followed by a suite of mourners. The King and Queen bring Princess Pirlipat to observe the executions. Krysilda, beside herself with grief and horror, swears to avenge these aristocrats' lives by casting a spell on the Princess. The King calls for Drosselmeyer to protect his daughter. Drosselmeyer introduces mousetraps and cats to keep the rats away from Pirlipat.

М. Шемякин.
2002г.

Балет С. Слонимского
и К. Симонова.

"Принцесса
Пирлипат
или Наказанное
Благородство."

Эскиз костюма
стражницы.

Балет „Принцесса Пирлипат".
Муз. С.Слонимского.
Крысоловы.
(Шествие.)
I акт.
I-ая Картина.

I акт. I-зя Картина.
Балет „Пирлипат."

М.Шемякин. 2001г.

М.Шемякин.
2002г.

Маска
юного
Котика.
сцена
„Донжон."

Маска маленького Кота.   (Сцена „Донжон.")

М.Шемякин.
2002г.

Эскиз костюма
Криса из буржуазного
общества.

Балет С. М. Слонимского
« Д. Самонова
« Принцесса Пирлипат
или
Наказанное благородство.»

Акт I.ый Картина IV-ая

(Боннсен.)

М. Шемякин-Кардановъ.

2002 г. Клаверак. U.S.A.

62

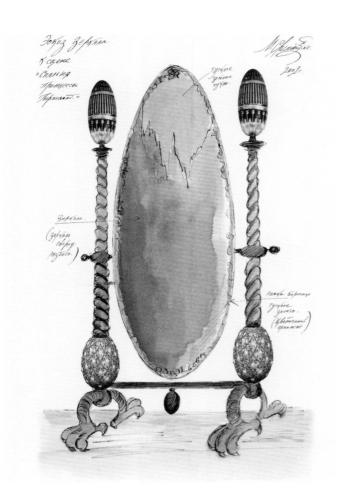

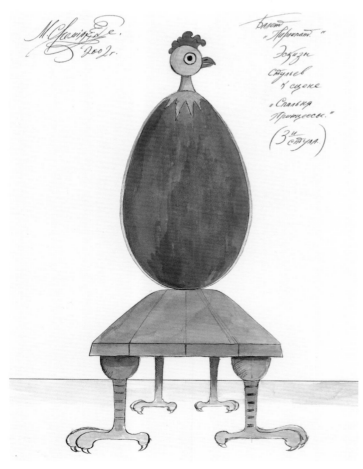

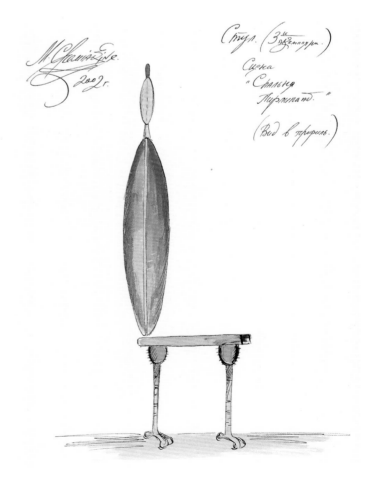

Act I. Scene 2.
Pirlipat's Bedroom

Sixteen years have passed since Krysilda's curse on the infant Pirlipat. The Princess pines in her heavily guarded bedroom, accompanied by her protectors, the cats, who have by now grown old and fat. The King comes to bid his daughter good night and check the room for intruders. He warns Pirlipat that danger is always near and that she must not take Krysilda's threats lightly. When he leaves, Pirlipat retires and the cats promptly doze off. Krysilda tiptoes into the bedroom, easily avoiding the sleeping cats. She leans into Pirlipat's bed and bites the Princess. A moment later, Pirlipat gets up, waking the cats. The beautiful Princess has been transformed into an ugly monster with a huge mouth—a Nutcracker. The cats, horrified by their lapse in protecting the Princess, try to flee the bedroom, but meet the King on the way. The King, seeing his daughter in such distress, is desperate to help her. He sends the cats for Herr Drosselmeyer.

Herr Drosselmeyer comes to the room with his nephew and encounters the King's accusations. It is Drosselmeyer's fault—the mousetrap and cat system has failed to protect Pirlipat. And Drosselmeyer caused the quarrel with the rats in the first place by accusing them of stealing the sausage. Drosselmeyer must reverse the spell on Pirlipat if he wishes to live.

Young Drosselmeyer, meanwhile, is moved by Pirlipat's trouble and tries to comfort her.

Herr Drosselmeyer reflects on the events and concludes that the only way to break the spell is with the help of the Magic Nut, Crackatook. He and his nephew set out on a journey to find Crackatook and bring it back to the kingdom.

Эскиз костюма
и маски
"Принцесса
Лулипит."
(Фрагмент
балет
С. Слонимского)

Балетъ „Пирлипатъ."

Эскизъ фигуры
украшающей
верхушку Кровати
Принцессы.
(2е Фигуры.)

Сцена „Спальня
Пирлипатъ."

Кровать Принцессы
Пирлипатъ.
(Сцена „Спальня
Принцессы.")

Въ кровати
прячутся
2е Актрисы.

Кресло-Тронъ.
(Тамъ должны
уместиться
2е Актрисы.)
Пологъ
долженъ
Закрываться
и
открываться.

Балетъ „Пирли-
патъ."
Сцена
Королевского
бала.

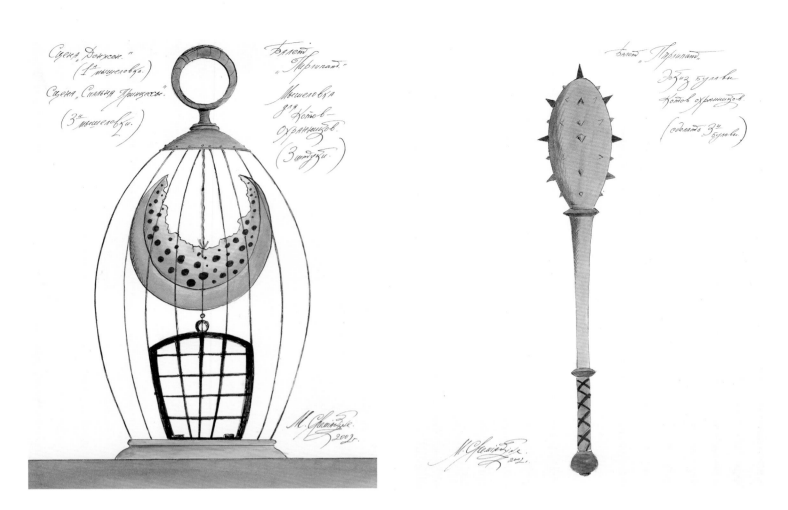

Сцена „Докисон.“
(1я мышеловка.)
Сцена „Спальня Принцессы.“
(3я мышеловки.)

Балет
„Тырюпат“.
Мышеловка
для „Котов-
охранников.
(3 штуки.)

Балет „Тырюпат“.
Эскиз булавы
Котов охранников.
(сделать 3я булавы)

Маска и Костюм к балету С.М.Слонимского:
"Волшебный орех."

"Медуза."
Сцена "Подводное Царство."

16 медуз
Б взрослых. 4 пары.
8 детей. 4 пары.

М.Скремицкая. 2005г.

Act I. Scene 3.
The Underwater Kingdom

*D*rosselmeyer and his nephew follow the nut to an underwater kingdom, where they are surrounded by terrifying witches, demons, and sea monsters. Warriors try to stop them by force, jellyfish threaten to entrap them, a voluptuous mermaid tempts Herr Drosselmeyer; and finally, when all else has failed, the whole population surrounds the visitors, trying to sell them souvenirs. At first the Drosselmeyers seem to be succumbing to this temptation of melancholy and gloom, but finally they remember their quest and disengage themselves from the seaweed and the witches' trawling nets and hurry off in pursuit of the nut Crackatook.

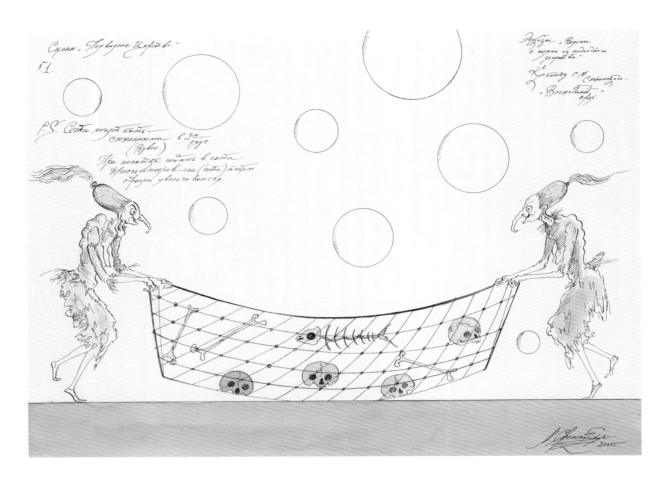

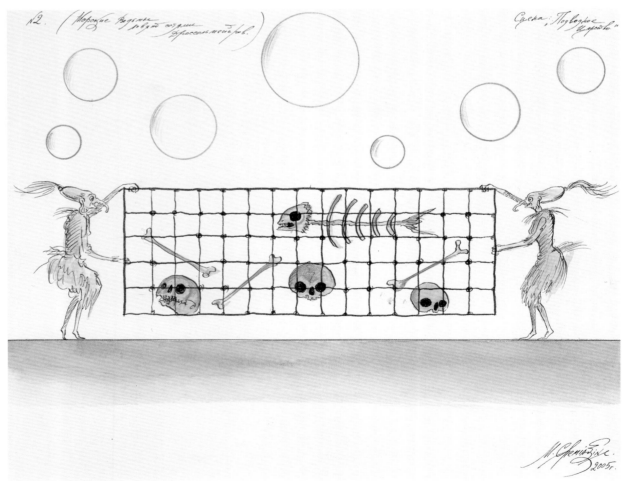

Эскиз костюма и маски
Подводной Ведьмы
к балету С.М. Слонимского
"Волшебный орех."
Сцена "Подводного царства."

Сцена „Подводное царство."

Эскиз „Морское чудище"
Балет С. М. Слонимского
„Волшебный орех."

М. Семякине.
2005.

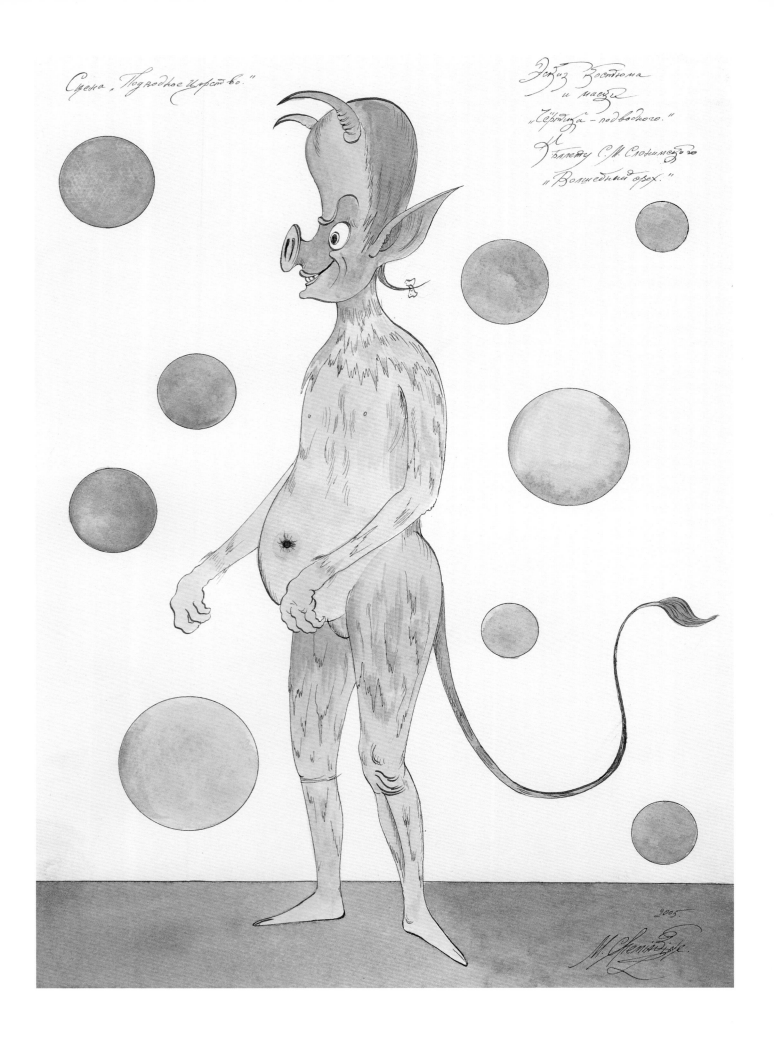

Сцена „Подводное Царство."

Эскиз Костюма
и маски
„Чёртика – подводного."

К балету С. М. Слонимского
„Волшебный орех."

2005.

80

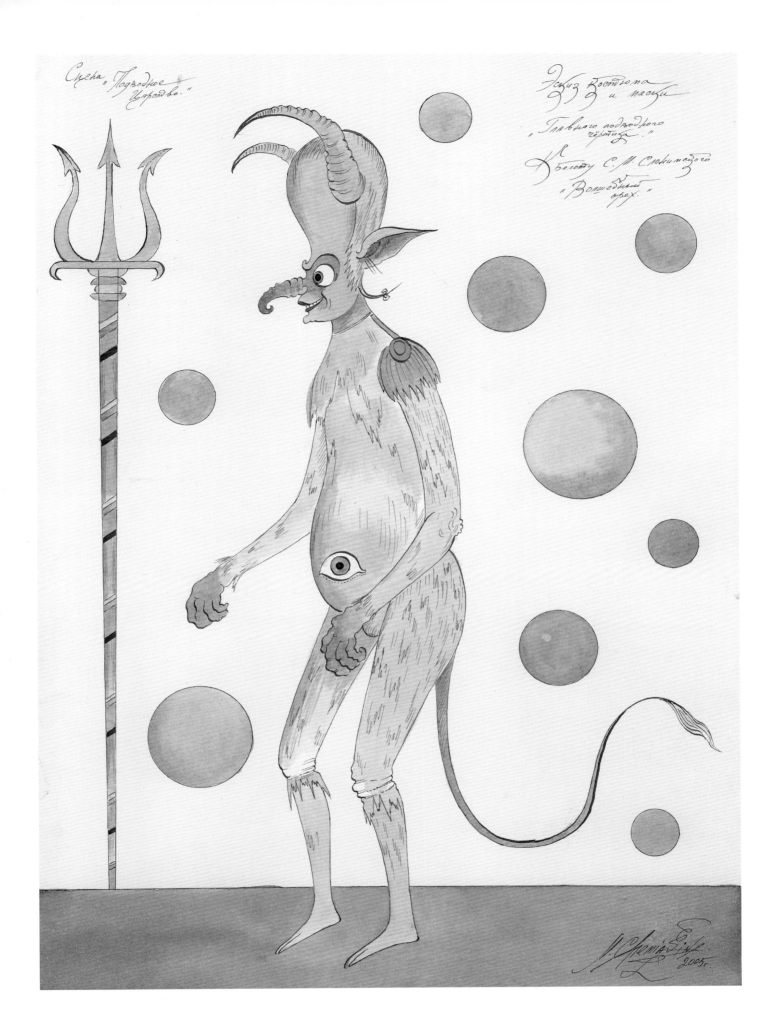

Сцена „Подводное Царство."

Эскиз костюма и маски „Главного подводного чёртика."

К балету С. М. Слонимского „Волшебный орех."

81

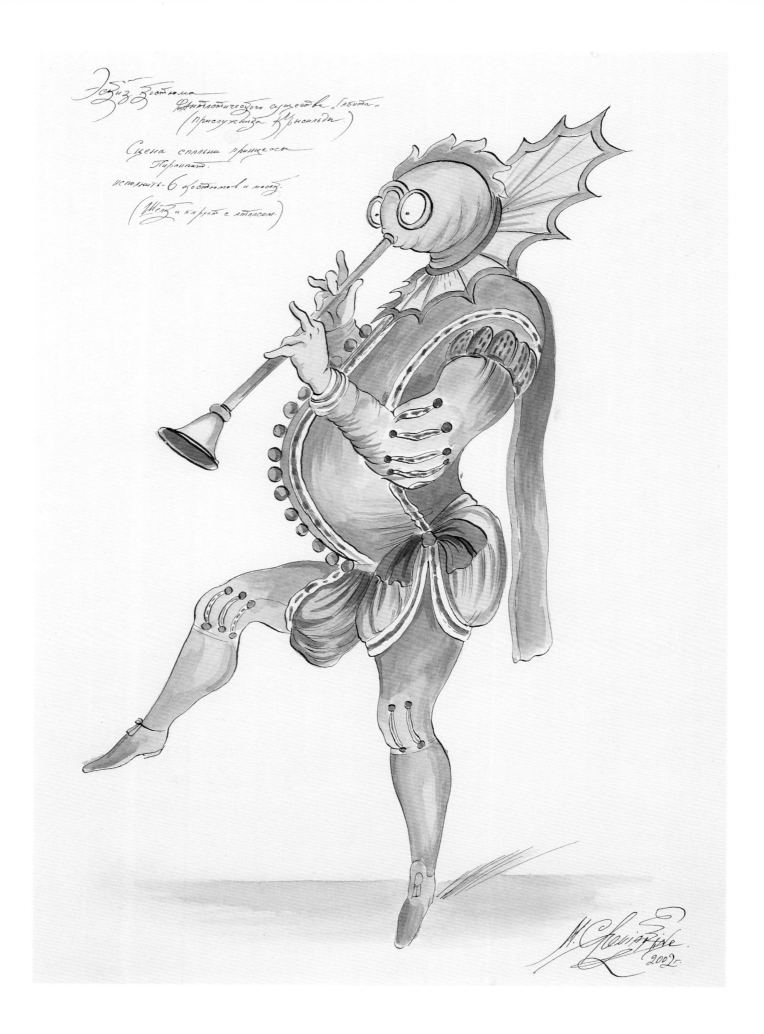

Эскиз костюма
фантастического существа „Габита"
(Прислужница Кунсильды.)

Сцена спальни принцессы
Пирлипат.
исполнить – 6 костюмов и масок.
(Шёлк и бархат с атласом.)

Эскиз костюма и маски
„Рыбка." (исп. Дети.)

к балету С. М. Слонимского
„Волшебный орех."

Сцена „Подводное
Царство."

(Маск.)

(Шелк—подсвечивающий.)

(6 персон.)
(Дети.)

Эскиз костюма и маски
к балету С.М. Слонимского
"Волшебный Орех."

"Морской Конёк."

Сцена "Подводное Царство."

Золотистый тюль
(Поблёскивающий.)

12 коньков.
(6 пар.)

Эскиз костюма
и маски
"Подводного монаха" —
к балету С. М. Слонимского
"Волшебный орех."

Сцена "Подводное
царство."

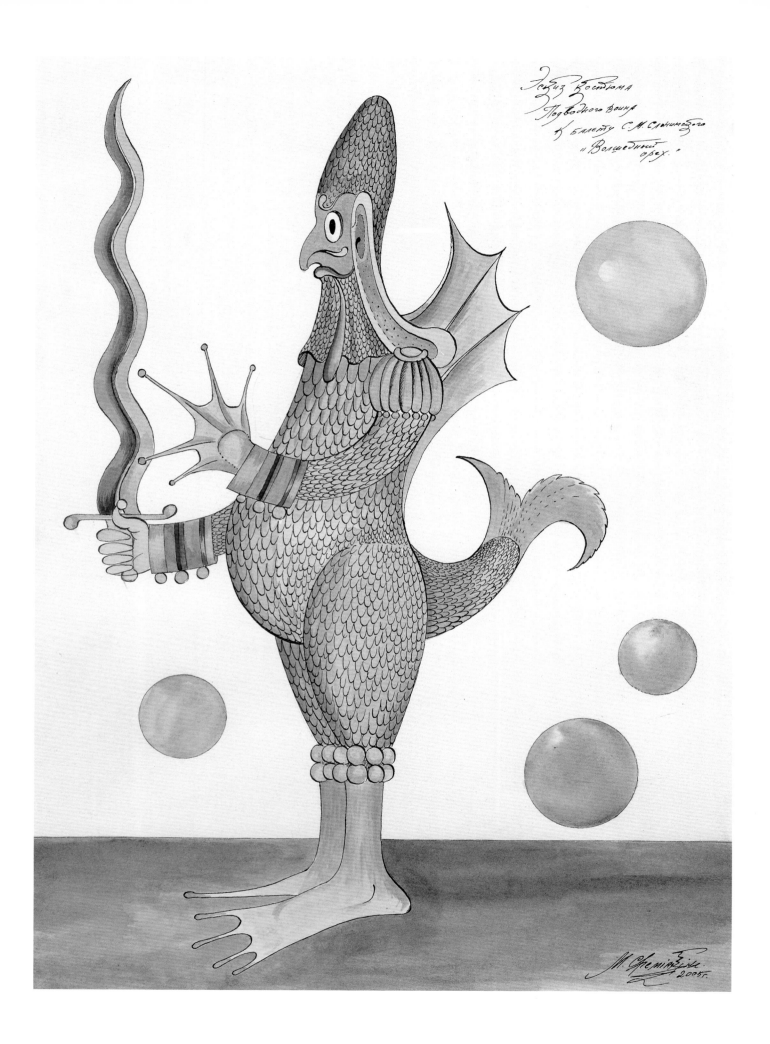

Эскиз костюма
Подводного
восклицателя

к балету С. М. Слонимского
"Волшебный орех."

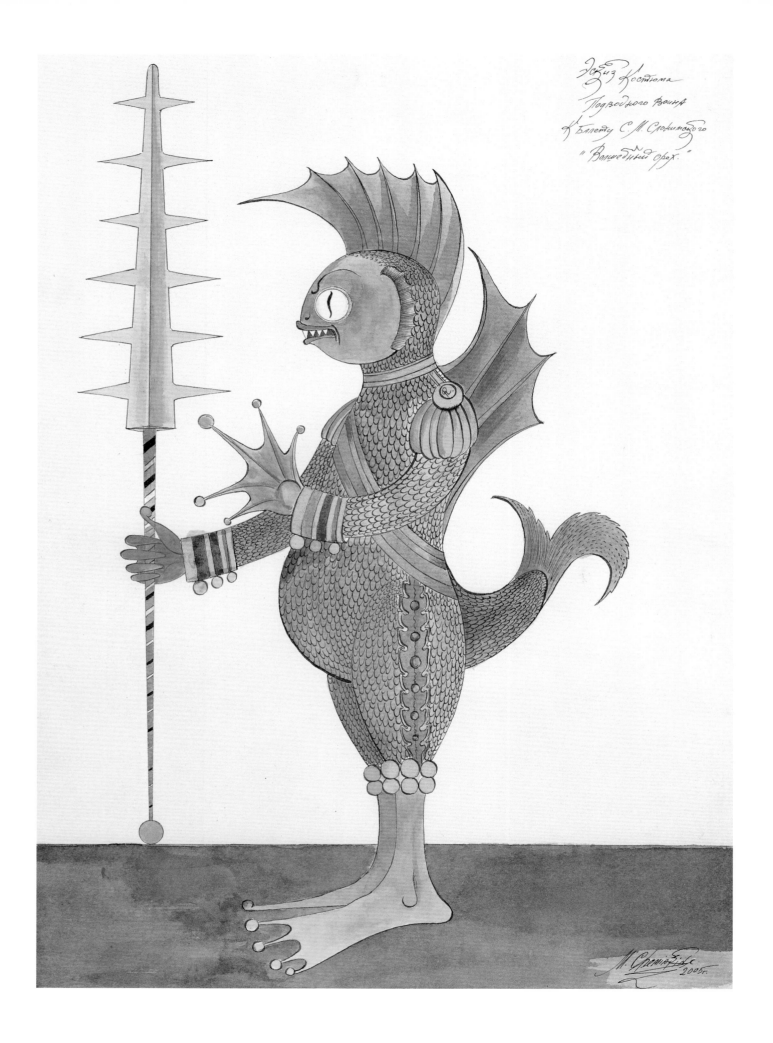

Сцена –
"Подводное
Царство."

Эскиз костюма
"Русалки-соблазнитель-
-ницы"

К балету. С. М.
Слонимского
– "Волшебный
орех."

92

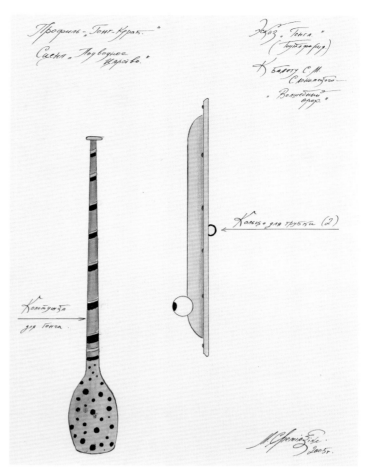

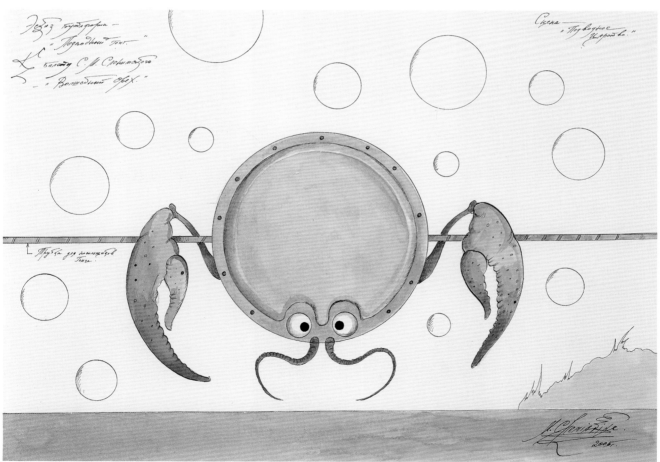

Эскиз — бутафории.
„Рак — леденец." I.
„Варёный рак." II
(вниз головой)
(На музыку „Китайский базар.")
К балету — С. М. Слонимского —
„Волшебный орех."
Сцена
„Подводное Царство."
2005 г.

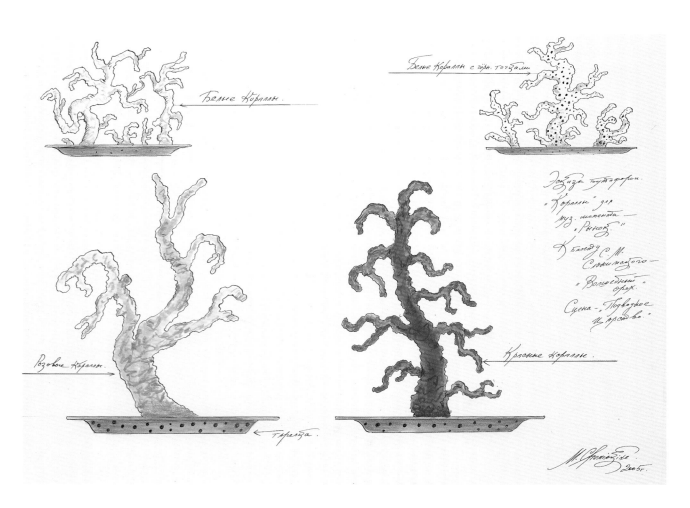

Белые Кораллы с гор. тотфами

Белые Кораллы.

Эскизы бутафории.
"Кораллы" для
муз. момента —
"Рынок".

К балету С. М.
Слонимского —
"Волшебный
орех."

Сцена — Подводное
царство.

Розовые Кораллы.

Красные Кораллы.

Тарелка.

Сцена "Подводное
царство."

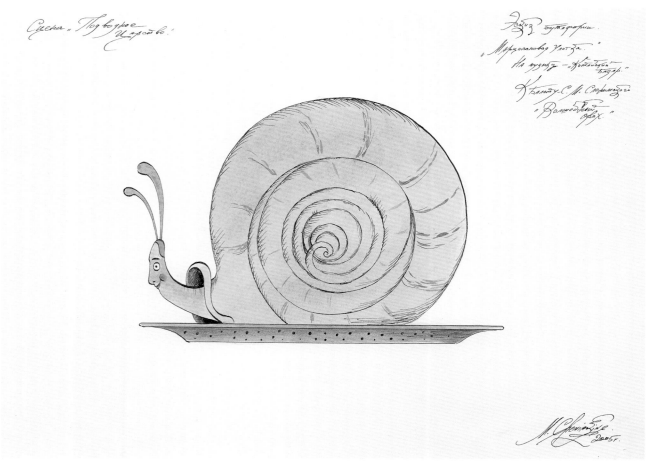

Эскиз бутафории.
"Мраморная Улитка."
На музыку — "Антилибеш
Бодар."

К балету С. М. Слонимского
"Волшебный
орех."

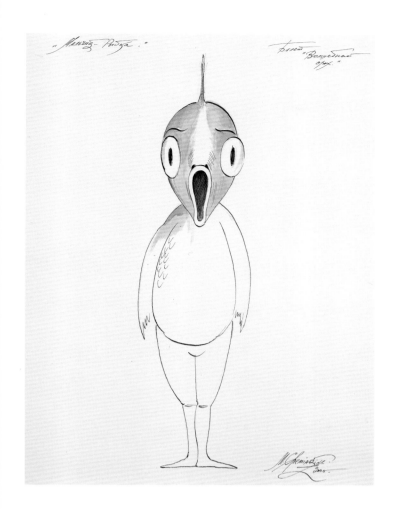

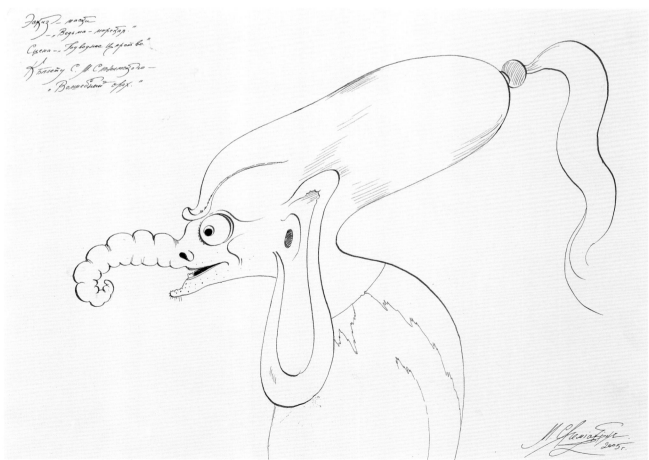

Облачное ложе-Кресло —
для младшего Дроссельмейера
к балету С. М. Слонимского —
"Волшебный Орех."

Сцена —
P.S.   "Искушение
(ложе стоит на заднем плане   Весельем."
на фоне – Небес и облаков.)

Act I. Scene 4.
The Kingdom of Merriment

Pursuing the nut Crackatook out from underwater, Drosselmeyer and his nephew find themselves in an aerie, on clouds populated by putti with beer and wine. Here all is merriment. Lovely girls and a Venus-like seductress invite the visitors to dance. Young men offer drink and good cheer. This is a kingdom where barrels of wine run after the drinkers, offering more refreshment. The visitors are at first inclined to remain here, forgetting their mission to recover the nut Crackatook, but spot a group of rats with the nut and rush off after them.

Сцена – „Искушение
Весельем."

(Парики – золотые.)
(Орнаменты – золото.)

Эскиз костюма и парика –
„Юноши – служителя
Бахуса",

К балету С. М.
Слонимского –
– „Волшебный
орех."

100

Эскиз костюма
и парика —
«Служительница Венеры.»
К балету С. М. Слонимского —
«Волшебный орех.»

Сцена «Искушение
Весель.»
(Парики — золотые.)
(Орнамент —
золото.)

М. Шемякин.
2005 г.

Костюм и парик
"Девушки-соблазнительницы"
К балету С. М.
Слонимского
"Волшебный
орех."

М. Шемякин
2005 г.

Сцена – „Искушение
Весельем."

1. Парик – золотой.
2. Крылья – золотые
3. Лук и стрелы – золотые.

Эскиз фигуры
„Купидона." к балету —
С. М. Слонимского —
„Волшебный орех."

М. Chemiakine.
2005.

103

Сцена —
"Искушение Весельем."

Костюм и маска
"Сатира."
К балету С.М.
Слонимского —
"Волшебный орех."

М. Шемякин
2005 г.

Эскиз костюма и маски
"Сатирши".
К балету С. М. Слонимского
— "Волшебный орех."

Сцена —
"Искушение
Весельем."

Костюм и маска "Пана."
К балету С. М. Слонимского —
"Волшебный орех."
Сцена "Искушение
Весельем."

P.S. Костюм — с
большими утолщениями
— проследить.

2005 г.

Эскиз фигуры
"Большого Бахуса."
К балету С. М. Слонимского-
- "Волшебный
орех."

Эскизы костюмов —
"бутафории."
...поля — вода.
К балету С. Любимского
"Волшебный орех."
Сцена —. "Искушение
Весельем."

Сцена "Искушение
Великим Весельем."

Эскиз бутафории —
"Голова в бочке с вином."
(Пьяница.) К балету
С. Любимского —
"Волшебный орех."

орех „Кракатук."
ширина 1 м. 15-20 см.
Высота — 1 м.

балет
„Щелкунчик."

Эскиз ореха —
— волшебнаго
„Кракатука."

Подставка —
сыр
(четырёх —
— сторонний)

Высота
пъедестала
2 м. 50 см.

Act II. Scene 1.
The Rat Kingdom

R ats of all kinds have gathered to fete their long-awaited revenge of their executed aristocrats. Crackatook, their trophy and the key to their victory, hangs overhead. Spanish, French, German rats entertain one another with national dances, the young hooligan rats whip the gathering into a frenzied celebration. Finally, the assembled company goes off to sleep.

Herr Drosselmeyer and his nephew sneak into the rats' meeting hall and make off with the Magic Nut. The elder Drosselmeyer explains to his nephew that the kernel from this nut will break the spell on Princess Pirlipat.

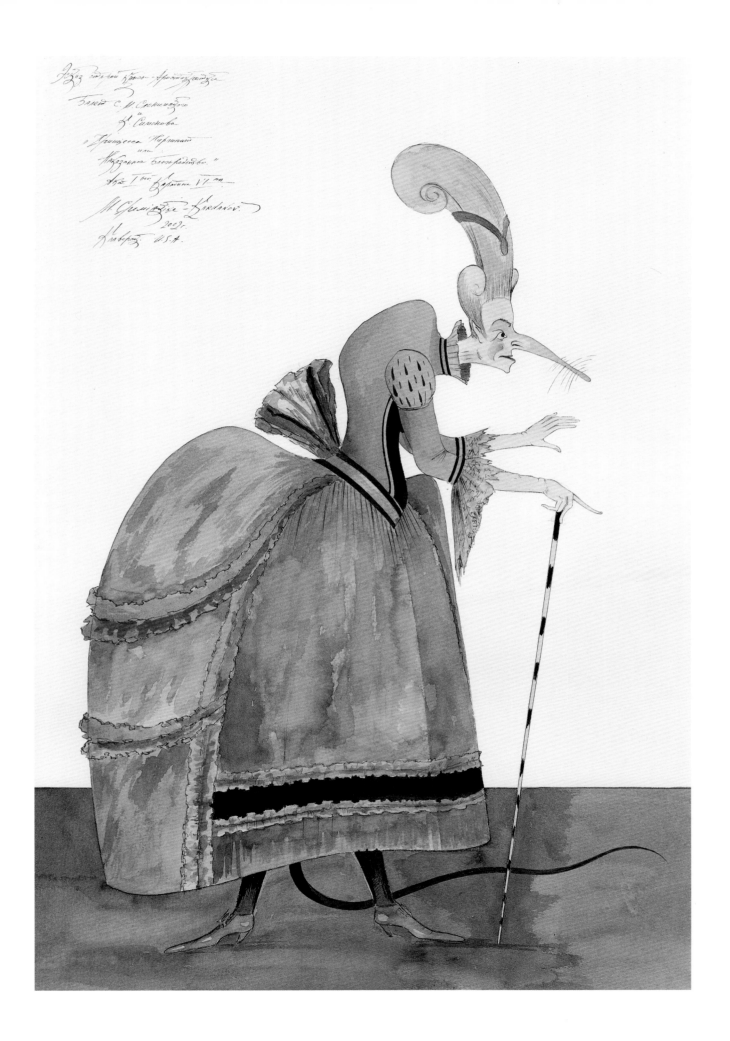

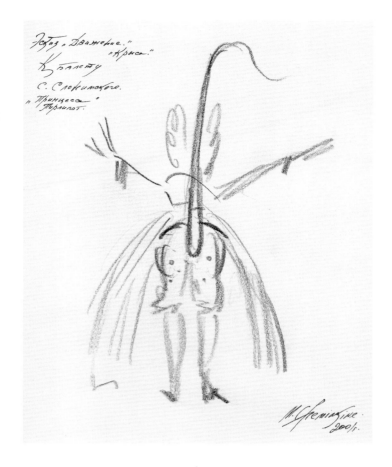

118

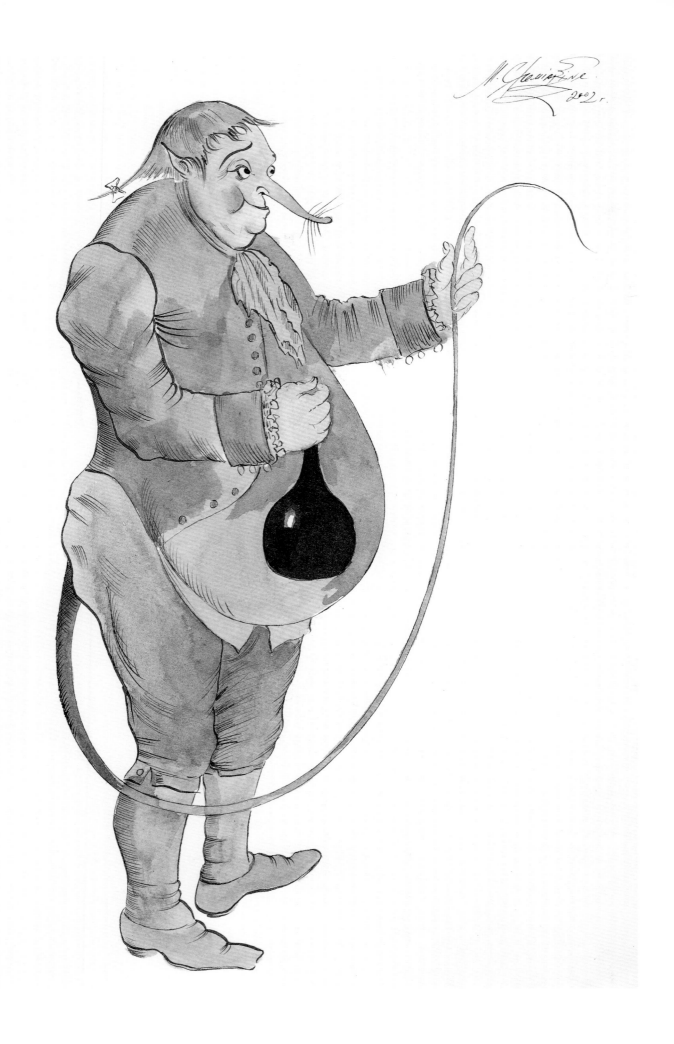

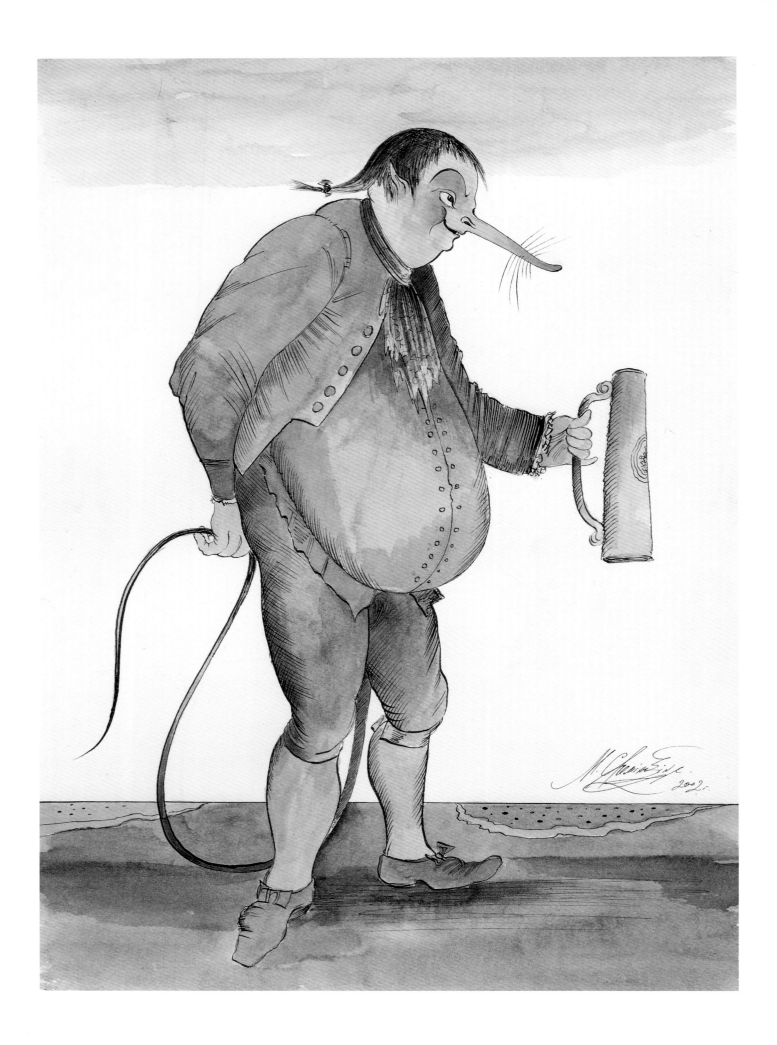

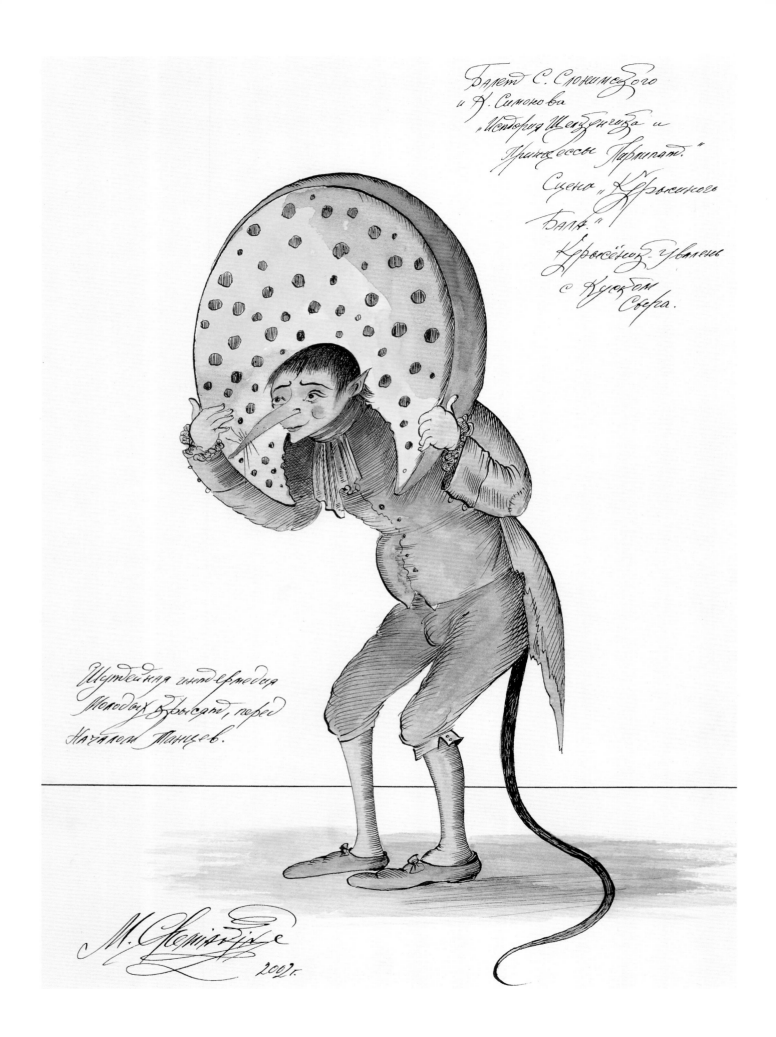

Балет С. Слонимского
и А. Симонова
"История Щелкунчика и
Принцессы Пирлипат."
Сцена "Крысиного
Бала."
Крысёнок-Увалень
с Куском Сыра.

Шутейная интермедия
Молодых Крысят, перед
началом Танцев.

М. Шемякин
2002 г.

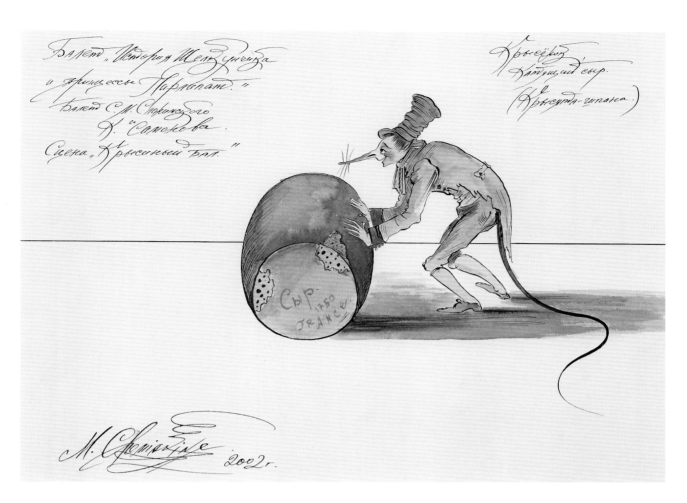

Балет „История Щелкунчика
и принцессы Пирлипат."
Балет С. М. Слонимского
К. „Самохова.
Сцена „Крысиный бал."

Крысёнок
Катящий сыр.
(Крысута-гигапа.)

М. Шемякин 2002 г.

Балет „Принцесса Пирлипат."
Сцена „Крысиный бал."
(Крысёнок (гигана)
Катит сыр.

Сцена буйства
молодых Крысят.
(Перед началом)
Танцев.

М. Шемякин 2002 г.

Эскиз Крысёнка с сыром.
Балет „Щелкунчик."
Сцена „Крысиный Бал."

М. Шемякин. 2001г.

Орех „Кракатук.“

М. Шемякин.
2002.

Act II. Scene 2.
The Royal Gardens: Pirlipat's Suitors

The King has prepared his gardens for the reception of suitors for Princess Pirlipat. He has announced that whoever cracks the Magic Nut will have her hand in marriage and inherit the kingdom. The monstrous Princess is hidden in a specially prepared throne, out of view of the suitors.

Young men have come from all over the world in hopes of winning the Princess' hand and the avian kingdom. One by one, they try to crack the nut. No one is able to, and it seems that all is lost. Then Herr Drosselmeyer asks the King to give his nephew a chance. To the astonishment of all present, young Drosselmeyer easily cracks the nut and hands the kernel to Pirlipat. The Princess emerges from her throne, restored to her former beauty.

Pirlipat dances with her savior. During their dance young Drosselmeyer accidentally bumps into a cloaked lady and knocks her to the ground. The lady's cloak falls off, revealing Krysilda. The rat Queen curses him, turning young Drosselmeyer into a Nutcracker, to the horror of the assembled guests. Princess Pirlipat recoils, then joins the courtiers in ridiculing the Nutcracker and banishing him from the kingdom along with his uncle.

Балет „Пирлипат."

6ая Картина.

(Королевский)
Бал.

Эскиз
Головного убора
для 4^{ех}
Женихов - Поляков.

— Темно зеленое.

— Красное.

— Чёрное.

М. Шемякин.

2002 г.

134

Балет
"Пирлипат"
6ая Картина.
(Королевский
Бал.
(МАЗУРКА.

Эскиз
Костюма
для 4^{ех}
Женихов-
Поляков.

(Танцуют
с принцессой
Пирлипат.)

135

пан бархат.
шёлк.

орнаменты тёмносиние
с золотыми.
(на бархате.)

шёлк.

шёлк.

Балет "Щелкунчик"

1.) Турок-жених.

Картина 6.ая

Королевский
бал.

М. Шемякин.
2002 г.

Эскиз костюма для турецкого жениха.
Балет С. Слонимского
"Принцесса Пирлипат"

М.Ш. 2002 г.

(Турецкий марш.)

(Танцуют с платками.)

Эскиз костюма

2) Турок-Жених.

Балет „Пирлипат.“

Сцена 6-ая

(Королевский бал.)

М. Шемякин.
2002 г.

панбархат.

шёлк.

орнамент — чёрный, вперемежку с тёмно-синим. (с вкраплением золота.)

шёлк.

шёлк

Эскиз костюма турецк. жениха
к балету С. М. Слонимского
„Принцесса Пирлипат“
М. Шемякин.
2002 г.

«Балет „Пырлипат."

6ая Картина.

„Королевский бал."

(Венгерский Танец.)

Тёмно синий мундир

Эскиз Костюма.
(Головной Убор.)

1 жених. (Венгр.)

чёрный цвет.

М. Шемякин.
2002 г.

Эскизи костюмов
2х
женихов-Венгров.
6ая
Картина.
(Королевский)
бал.

М. Шемякинъ.
2002 г.

Балет
„Принцесса
Пирлипат."

Картина 6ая
(Королевский
бал.)

(Тёмно синие
мундиры
с золотом.)

Эскиз Костюма
1го Жениха-Венгра.

М. Шемякин.
2002 г.

(Балет
„Пирлипат.")
Картина 6ая.
(Королевский
бал.)

Эскиз Костюма
2) Жених-Венгр.

М. Шемякин.
2002 г.

Балет „Принцесса
Пирлипат."
6ая Картина
(Королевский бал.)

Жёлтый
приглушённый
(мундир)
с чёрными
вставками.

Эскиз Костюма
3го Жениха-Венгра.

цвет
чёрный

М. Шемякин.
2002 г.

Балет „Принцесса
Пирлипат."
6ая Картина
(Королевский бал.)

Эскиз Костюма
4го Жениха-Венгра.
(Венгерский
танец.)

М. Шемякин.
2002 г.

Костюм
Принцессы
Пирлипат.
сцена 5ая
СПАЛЬНЯ
Принцессы.

Балет „Пирлипат"

(Волосы — Чёрные.)

М. Шемякинъ.
2002г.

М. Шемякинъ.
2002.

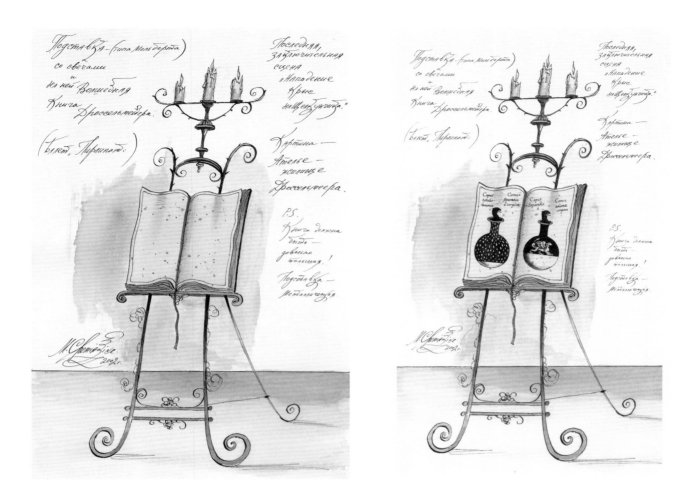

Act II. Scene 3.
Drosselmeyer's Workshop

Drosselmeyer, discouraged by the turn of events, is deep in his calculations when Cardinal Kryselieu arrives to gloat. The two sorcerers make a bet over who will determine young Drosselmeyer's fate.

The Nutcracker arrives, pining for Pirlipat. He replays their waltz, recalling how happy he was just a short time ago. But the Princess is only a painful memory for him. The enchanted young man slowly stiffens, turning to wood, as a division of rat gendarmes rushes in to attack him. Drosselmeyer protects his nephew as well as he can.

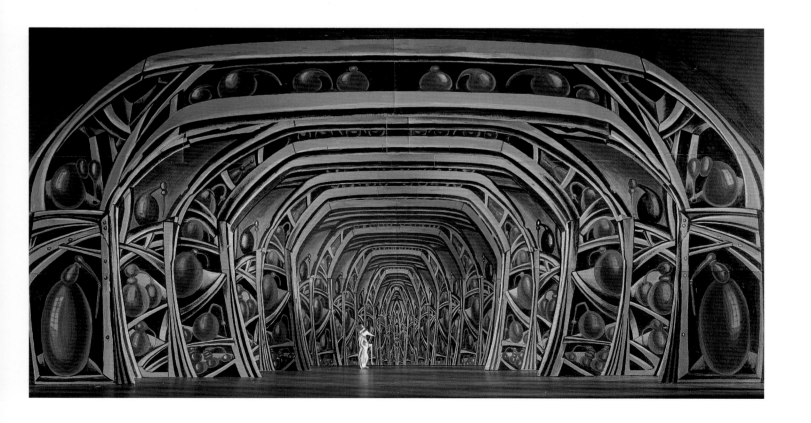

Балет
«Прилипат.»
(Заключительная)
сцена.

Эскиз костюма

Начальница
стражи
(Жандармов-)
Крыс.

Видео еранцы.

М. Шемякин
2002г.

Балет „Щелкунчик".
Заключительная сцена.

Эскиз костюма

Начальника
Крысиной стражи.

(Перчатки - бело-серые.)

М. Шемякин.
2002 г.

Балетъ „Щелкунчикъ."

(Заключительная
Картина.)

Эскизъ костюма
рядового-Жандарма-
-Крыса.

(Видъ въ профиль.)

М. Шемякинъ. 2002г.

Балет
„История Щелкунчика
и
Принцесса Пирлипат."

Заключительная
сцена.

(Нападение
Крыс-жандармов
на
Щелкунчика.)

Рядовой-
Жандарм-
Крыс.

М. Шемякин.
2002 г.

Finale

*H*err Drosselmeyer is introduced to a young girl, Masha, and her brother Fritz. He shows them a Nutcracker doll like the one the rats tried to give to Princess Pirlipat, and is pleased to see that Masha is delighted by the doll. Herr Drosselmeyer has found the way to break the spell on his nephew.

About the Author

Mihail Chemiakin was born in Moscow in 1943, grew up in occupied East Germany, and returned to Russia in 1957 where he was admitted to the Special High School of the Repin Academy of Art in Leningrad. He was expelled from art school for failing to conform to Socialist Realist norms, and from 1959–1971 worked as a laborer in various capacities. He was subjected to compulsory treatment at a mental institution, which was a standard way of dealing with ideological dissidents at that time. For five years he worked on the maintenance crew of the Hermitage Museum. In 1967, the artist founded the St. Petersburg Group and developed the philosophy of Metaphysical Synthesism, dedicated to the creation of a new form of icon painting based on the study of religious art of all ages and peoples.

In 1971 Chemiakin was forced out of the USSR by the Soviet authorities. He settled first in France, then moved to New York City in 1981. While in Paris he edited and published *Apollon-77*, an almanach of post-Stalinist art, poetry, and photography in which many of the "non-conformists" were first published. Chemiakin also recorded and published the first disks of gypsy singers Vladimir Poliakoff and Aliocha Dmitrievich, both of whom lived in Paris. He worked for several years with Russian bard Vladimir Vysotsky, systematically recording his songs for what became a seven-record set of Vysotsky's music. Chemiakin continues to publish books and music by under-recognized artists under the aegis of the Apollon Art Research Foundation.

In 1989, the return of Chemiakin's work to post-Communist Russia began with the first exhibition of his work there since his exile. Subsequently, he continued to show his work there and has installed four monuments in St. Petersburg, to *Peter the Great*, to the *Victims of Political Repressions*, to the *Architects and Builders of St. Petersburg*, and to assassinated deputy mayor M. Manevich. Chemiakin's *Cybele: Goddess of Fertility* stands in New York's SoHo. A variation on the monument to Peter the Great is on permanent display in Normandy. In 1998 Chemiakin's *Monument to Giacomo Casanova* was installed in Venice in honor of the bicentenary of Casanova's death. *Dialogue between Plato and Socrates*, a memorial to Professor Harold Yuker, is installed at Hofstra University in New York; a monument to actor Savely Kramarov stands in San Francisco. In 2001 monuments were installed in Moscow, *Children - Victims of the Sins of Adults* and in London, *Peter the Great* (marking the tercentenary of Peter I's visit to Deptford).

The research begun in the 1960s into the art of all ages and peoples has developed into a collection of millions of images organized into technical, historical, and philosophical categories that has earned the artist five Honorary Doctorates and is the basis for his Institute of the Philosophy and Psychology of Art. The Russian "Kultura" channel produced a series of thirteen programs featuring Chemiakin and his research in 2002–2003.

Chemiakin's first theatrical work was at the Rimsky-Korsakov Conservatory in St. Petersburg (then Leningrad) in 1967. He designed a production of Shostakovich's opera-bouffe *The Nose* which was, as everyone expected, closed down by the authorities immediately after the premiere. Thirty-four years later Chemiakin's first ballet production, *The Nutcracker*, premiered across Theater Square from the Conservatory, at the Mariinsky Theater, and has played since 2001 in St. Petersburg, Moscow, Paris, Washington, D.C., and Baden-Baden.